ALMOST SOLD

THE MIRACLES GOD PERFORMED TO FREE ME FROM SEX SLAVERY

RACHEL LOUISE

WESTBOW
PRESS
A DIVISION OF THOMAS NELSON

WestBow Press books may be ordered through booksellers or by contacting:

WestBow Press
A Division of Thomas Nelson
1663 Liberty Drive
Bloomington, IN 47403
www.westbowpress.com
1-(866) 928-1240

ISBN: 978-1-4497-9453-8 (sc)
ISBN: 978-1-4497-9455-2 (hc)
ISBN: 978-1-4497-9454-5 (e)

Library of Congress Control Number: 2013908200

Printed in the United States of America.

WestBow Press rev. date: 07/15/2013

Special thanks to Jennifer, Julie, Courtney and Karen: My heart doesn't have adequate words of thanks and love for your support through the years.

I want to dedicate this book to those that God used in my life to help me get to this place of proclaiming His miracles . . . from the wonderful gal who ate at California Pizza with me that first day of sharing, to my two brunch pals cheering me on to continue. I love you.

TABLE OF CONTENTS

FOREWORD

This book is a shouting of His miracles. It is the story of God's movement to save my life from becoming one caught in a life of sexual abuse, God's saving my life from becoming one potentially lost in a foreign country, and God's redemption of my life to bring me to fullness and healing. Sex trafficking is not a new concept. Attention to this social injustice seems to have wonderfully caught fire in recent years, and the fire for freedom is spreading rapidly. This book is 10% description of the terror I went through, and 90% description of God's miracles from day one until today. Changes to names and places were made to ensure the safety of all involved.

My heart's desire is that everyone who reads this book is empowered by the Holy Spirit as there is agreement in Truth to the miraculous ways that God saved me. Read and Worship

Him with me in what He has wonderfully done! And if you have experienced this indefinable violation, I pray you hold onto His truth and love tightly. I pour my heart out for you to be encouraged in His love in order to take one more step forward.

Chapter 1

THE SETUP

The Lure.

His Lie.

My Loss.

I am an average American girl. Growing up, my life included things like church on Sundays, fireworks on the Fourth of July, and the neighborhood swim team. I was a shy extrovert who yearned for adventure, but I also wanted to please my parents and teachers.

I was a rule-follower by nature, though I did have one "wild child" adventure in high school when I snuck out one night with my best friend to see a band play in a bar/sandwich shop named Ducky's. This was when we experienced our first cigarette.

I was so worried about being caught that I never snuck out again. I had good friends, made A's and B's in school, and was in student council. After high school, I attended an average private Christian college where I joined a sorority and volunteered at a nursing home. However, things soon took a tailspin. Two months after graduating from college, I found myself caught in a dark, evil place with a man who consistently abused me.

What happened? How could this have happened to me? How did I, a normal, sweet Christian girl, find myself completely alone in an unfamiliar city—hurt from consistent sexual and mental abuse meant to obliterate my self-will, with a man I hated and feared? How did the girl who still had pink walls and lace curtains at her parent's house slip into such a dark place? How did my reality become a question of if I would be sold in a foreign country—or die?

I used to have this idea for how I wanted my career to look. In high school, I remember going into the Bombay Company store and deciding that my future office furniture would be cherry tree wood. Back then I decided on rich maroon leather couches and gold lamps for the desks. I wanted to take a subway to work, with a Starbucks in one hand and *The Wall Street Journal* in the other, sporting a long, black pea coat to complement my refined look. I wanted to be a powerful force, maybe an expert in something.

When I received the opportunity to move to New York after college, I thought that my chance at my dream had arrived. The job was entry level, and the pay was peanuts, but I knew this was the chance I had been waiting for. This job would help me embrace the real me: sophisticated, capable, and successful.

Packing my car as full as possible, I filled up with gas, grabbed a map, and said good-bye to my family. The Lord says in Matthew 10:16, "Therefore be as shrewd as snakes and as innocent as doves." I had the innocence part down, believing the good in people and actually taking them at their word. The shrewdness of a snake, or as stated in other Bible translations, being "wise as a serpent," was where I had some learning and refinement to do. So many times I had wished I could go back in time and shake wisdom into my twenty-one–year-old self.

THE LURE

It started for him with the first time we met. It started for me with a kiss. Through a work connection, I met Hassan, a businessman in his late thirties. I approached the situation very professionally, wanting to prove myself as a businesswoman, and this happened to be my very first client meeting. He was gregarious and warm in his Jay Kos tailored suit. I remember thinking that I couldn't have scripted our meeting any better; we both wanted to pursue a business connection between our companies that would be mutually beneficial.

As we got to know each other in this first business meeting, I shared offhandedly with him that my employer was looking for a new office for me in the city. Our lease had not been renewed by our landlord, and we had five weeks until I got the boot. My boss had given me the task of finding a new place to rent. I vented to Hassan that I was irked; my degree was not in real estate and I had no idea how to get a commercial lease. He said that he happened to know a person who could help me out. Hassan explained that he used to be an adjunct professor at one of the City University of New York (CUNY) community college campuses. Since I used student volunteers for my "staff," he said that he might be able to get me a space in one of the offices in the college and couch it as a student group.

I thought that I had hit the jackpot. The pressure to perform for my boss with both hands tied behind my back started to ease. And, as luck would have it, Hassan mentioned he was meeting with one of the deans that next Monday morning and could pitch the idea to him. He suggested that we get together to discuss it that Thursday. We parted ways that afternoon with normal pleasantries, and I could not wipe the smile off my face. I called my co-worker at the other city location to share the news. She was thrilled and said that she would come with me to the business meeting on Thursday.

On Thursday afternoon, I got a call from my co-worker; she discovered that she had accidentally double-booked herself that evening. There was a junior league outreach at a local library and she had RSVP'ed for me and her to go. I was not a member of the junior league, but the longing for a social evening out rather than sitting at home by myself gave me the courage to attend anything as a guest. I really wanted to go to the library outreach. I didn't think that waiting a day on the business meeting would hurt anything, so I decided it could wait. I called Hassan and told him that we needed to reschedule, and we reset the meeting for Friday.

Still on a buzz from the night before and feeling like I finally had some kind of social life, Friday came with new courage for me. I felt like I was starting to get into my groove. I had a skip in my step of extra optimism that life was going to work out after all.

Later that Friday, my co-worker called me to tell me that her boyfriend had surprised her with tickets to Vermont. She would need to leave that night for the weekend. I was excited for her; I could tell that she could use a break from work for a while. It did not dawn on me until the end of the workday that the meeting with Hassan would have to be rescheduled yet again.

I called and left a message for Hassan telling him I needed to reschedule, then left for the day to head home. As soon as I got home, Hassan called my cell phone. He said that the meeting with the dean was set for Monday and he wasn't sure when he would be able to schedule another meeting. If I wanted to explain what my office needed space-wise and give a rundown of what it was exactly that we did for the dean to consider, I would need to meet him that night.

An instant red flag popped up, but one that I could not put my finger on. Something did not feel right about this situation. It was indeed rushed, but wasn't Hassan doing a favor for me?

I became caught up in the concept that this was the one and only time he would ever be able to meet with the dean and that only the dean could help me get a new space for the office. I now know how this was a first test run for Hassan gauging my susceptibility to manipulation. If I had been more experienced, I might have known better than to fall for the "only solution" trick and the ticking clock he put on it.

Common sense said that it was never a good idea to meet a man for dinner alone that you don't know. Though I had met Hassan, I knew he could have been anybody and capable of anything.

Then again, perhaps I was acting paranoid. What would be the odds that this man had evil intentions? I brushed off my misgivings. Perhaps I was just nervous; this was, after all, my first real business connection and my first real business dinner. The circumstances seemed to be unique enough to excuse away my internal warnings. All of these thoughts went through my head in about three seconds, and to not prolong an already awkward pause, I told Hassan that I would meet him at the restaurant that we had agreed upon earlier that day. To be on the safe side, I called my boss to give her an update of the situation.

She complimented me on my resourcefulness and said that I was doing well with the curveball they threw me. I was excited to get this praise; I certainly didn't want to disappoint my boss now by letting feelings of intimidation get in the way of potentially a great deal. Besides, this was a business meeting, not a rendezvous at some loud nightclub.

The next words that I said to my boss before leaving should have been another red flag that I was not to go. I said, "It should be fine. I mean, he is married, nothing can happen." I knew the feeling in my gut as I spoke those words. It was the slightly sickening, growing unease of the Holy Spirit's stern warning. I did not have the experience to know how to discern if the Holy Spirit was telling me not to go, or if the Holy Spirit was warning me to be careful in going. I also did not have the experience to err on the side of caution when there are dangerous consequences at stake.

My boss asked if I was worried about something happening. To save face, I said of course not, and promised a summary of my proposal with his business the next Monday. I was unsure of what exactly she meant by "something happening". I only knew that I had quite a bit of unease, and speaking out loud that he was married was meant to appease this rise of warning that I did not understand. My pride became entangled in this first business arrangement working well. I did not want to be the reason it failed, and I did not want to be proven unable to make it in the NY business world. I have since learned that the opposite is quite true. There is room for calculated risk in business for opportunity, but if it comes with a risk to personal safety, it is never something anyone should endure in order to be truly successful. With the blessing of sorts from my boss, I left to meet Hassan at the restaurant.

It was dark by this time. Between trying to decipher the directions from my car's overhead light, to walking a few blocks alone in the dark from my parking spot, I was flustered before I even stepped foot into the restaurant. Once inside, I spotted Hassan at a table at the other end of the room. He was sitting with two other people that appeared to be the same nationality as he. As I approached, I noticed they all had the same thick accents. I was visually annoyed at how unprofessional it felt for him to have brought two random people to our business meeting, as if I had all the time in the world to waste. I didn't want to be rude, however, so I pretended, and smiled, and would nod politely as they finished whatever it was they were discussing.

The four of us engaged in random small talk for over half an hour. At one point the topic of conversation turned to religion. Hassan pulled out a rosary and said he always used it as a guide in his life. Encouraged at his openness to God, I shared that I was a Christian. I had no idea that this was not just random conversation to him. He was already methodically getting data about me to see if I was a good hit. Eventually the small talk ended and his friends left. Hassan and I were finally alone to discuss the business that we had come to discuss.

Before I could get a word out, I noticed him staring at me in a very odd way. I was a baffled at this entire evening. I wanted to just be done with this encounter and go home. Sheepishly, Hassan said "I like you Rachel. You are beautiful, and I have been wanting to tell you all night that I really like you." Instantly two worlds of thought went through my mind at the same time. The first was that I was thrilled to hear those words. I longed for affection deeply, and to be told I was beautiful. Being told I was liked by an adult man felt amazingly wonderful.

The second thought was more practical. I remembered he had said he was married. I was at a loss in this moment, and I am sure my face gave me away. Hassan quickly changed the subject back to business. Going along with the ridiculousness of the evening, I also went back to the topic of business as if he had not just expressed this sentiment. We talked for a little while, but because of all of the delays, the restaurant ended up closing before we ever got to anything substantial.

As we left, he gave indication that he realized it was late and that we just needed to get things wrapped up for

Monday's meeting. He suggested that we go back to his office downtown to get the papers we needed to sign. To this day, I still have no idea what papers he was talking about. I was too self-conscious to ask. Of course I know now that there were no papers. There aren't "papers" required to agree to recommend another business by word of mouth, and any information I would want the Dean to know for the potential office space would have come from me, not Hassan. I had just assumed Hassan was working without an ulterior motive. I assumed he did not have any reason for being anything but honest in our purpose of business.

We got into my car and left for his office. Like many people in New York, he did not have a car. Once we arrived, I could tell he was trying to impress me with his career status, making it seem like he was some big shot with his name etched in glass on the door. He began to look around for the papers. He told me to sit while he looked. His office was a plain windowless room with so much clutter, I thought he might have just moved in. While I was busy looking for a place to sit that did not have a stack of clutter on it, he bent over and surprised me with a kiss on my lips. I tensed. What was going on? He pulled away laughing at my reaction, and said he would try that again by the end of the night.

While he went on to shuffle through things on his desk, all I could think about was the fact that he was married. I started to bargain with God . . . I wanted to feel love so much. So deeply. I thought one simple kiss would not hurt anything, right? I begged God in my mind to please let him kiss me again, just once, just so I could feel loved! I knew I would be forgiven tomorrow. I was torn between what I knew was a huge line not to cross, and what my heart was telling me it *needed* to feel alive. 1 Corinthians 6:18 starts with the stern instruction to "Flee from sexual immorality". Flee! I did not realize how dangerous this was.

This was the key turning point, and Hassan knew it. What if I had lived out God's instruction? What if I stood up, said this is unacceptable, and walked out of his office? What if I proceeded to get into my car and just drive home?! That would be the end of this book! Instead, I actually thought I could get the dangling carrot of feeling loved for just a moment in front of me, and still not have any kind of real consequence. Hassan never tried to kiss me the rest of the night. He didn't need to, he already got the information he needed—that I had a deep longing for love he could use to exploit me.

He said that he did not have the papers that he needed and that instead, they were at his other business. He owned a business dealing with children in a bad part of town. At that point I wanted to just finish this business deal so I could be done with this whole thing and just go home. We got back into my car and started to drive toward the other business. I turned the car CD player on, and loud music started to blare. I had an angry, heavy metal rock band playing in my CD player. He asked me why I was so angry, motioning to the car CD player. I told him I didn't know, maybe issues with my parents. Hassan then asked how angry I was, and suddenly it felt like a dare to tell him the truth, a dare to shock him with my reality. I told him I was angry enough engage in self injury in the past.

I didn't know this guy from Adam, and I was telling him my deepest secrets. In that moment I knew something was increasingly wrong that I would tell a perfect stranger something like that. The sooner I was done with this night and home the better. We got to his office area and I parked the car. As we walked up to the building, I stepped on an empty crack vile, the glass crunching under my shoe. Because we were in a dangerous part of town, he locked the doors and set the alarm when we walked inside. I didn't think anything of it at the time. He put two chairs, facing each other, in the middle of the floor.

HIS LIE

The foundation was laid emotionally to manipulate and control me. Hassan was like a surgeon in how precise his moves were made. Continuous observations led him to make assumptions, and he had the confidence to speak those assumptions as if he knew everything about me as fact. He gathered clues to what made me vulnerable and then went in for the kill by offering the promise of ointment for the wound. He knew which wounds to pay attention to, how they tied to my significance, and what my heart longed for as a consequence. He said that we were going to sit down and get to the bottom of why I was so angry.

A part of me was thrilled, and incredibly relieved, that someone was listening to me and actually took what I was saying seriously. His care was intoxicating. We sat down across from each other, our knees about six inches apart facing each other. Except rather than talk, he begin touching me. I was very confused. Methodically he pushed the line, getting closer to crossing it inch by inch. I began to feel like it was a movie or a dream, not really happening to me.

I became lulled farther and farther, in a dream state as I crossed a line I didn't want to cross, then another, still convinced I was watching a movie of my life. A panic began to rise in me. In one split second I realized that: 1—the door was locked with keys he had. 2—he was playing and manipulating me at a level that terrified me and I was ineffective at making myself wake up to reality at that moment. 3—instinctively I knew not to make him angry. Reality crashed back instantly when I felt him trying to have sex with me. The act of sex had always been something I held as sacred. This was something that couldn't be manipulated from me. I was very certain to my core that I would not engage in that act before I was married; I wanted to keep it as a gift I could give to my husband. I pushed Hassan away, refusing. He decided that no was not an acceptable answer to him and forced it.

MY LOSS

In the morning, when I realized what he had done, I stared in shock at the reality that I was not a virgin anymore sank in. I started crying. He said "it's not your fault. God doesn't fault us for things that are not in our control. I always get what I want Rachel . . . I saw you and I wanted you. So I took you." I stared at him in disbelief. The words coming out of his mouth did not make sense. The tone of his voice held a small sliver of something resembling compassion, but the words that I heard were so vile in meaning, surely this is not a fellow human being. What had I just gone through?

The words he said left a foul odor in the air. For a short second, I wondered if the words could be erased—sucked from the air around us. Could the earth be forced to halt on its axis and be redirected? His words, *I always get what I want . . . and I wanted you, so I took you . . .* said as if I am supposed to understand this logic. Something sacred was ripped away the night before, and he was sitting next to me pouring acid into my wound by explaining his selfishness and labeling the piece of lust I was to him. A combination of hatred and fear began growing exponentially in my chest, replacing the overwhelming feeling of loss. When I found my voice, I said quietly, "Get away from me. I am never going to see you again."

His face turned from slight selfish compassion to completely enraged. He yelled in a controlled staccato of bursts. "Don't ever say that again! I *own* you now! You are MINE!"

At this, my mind began the process of dissociation. This reality was too much for me to handle. The amount of danger I was in could not register in my mind. He turned and got out of my car; and in shock I went back to the place I was living.

I can't remember what I did the rest of that day, I can't remember the next time I saw him, I can't even remember the days following. I know that I saw him sometime that next week, but I have no idea why. I know he wanted to come into the room that I rented, see where I lived. Days went by, and the next thing that I remember clearly is letting him come over to my place.

My heart could not take the truth of what had happened. It was a crushing horror. I came up with this idea that if I was in a "relationship" with Hassan, I could force the memory from one of trauma to one of consent, and I would not have been raped. Committing a sin was something I could deal with, being in danger for my life was not. I tried to convince myself that we were an "us" by allowing him over. I tried to convince myself that I didn't care about sex. I tried to forget the sacred place it held in my heart. And, I decided to have sex, as millions do every day, with the person I was "seeing".

None of these fantasies worked. He came over, and I tried to pretend, but I did not feel anything. Instead I ran on instinct which was telling me to go back home as soon as I could—before any more of a hole was dug. My mind had hundreds of thoughts per minute racing through it while he was with me that night. Now I just wanted him to leave so that I could run far from this whole thing. I listened to how silent the night was . . . how long until the sun came up and he left?

When the sun finally came up that next morning, while he was still in my bed, the man who rented the room across the hall from mine in the boarding house tried to break into my room. I had my door locked with a chain. He opened the door the two inches it would go and tried to break the chain. He was very drunk. I could not believe this was happening, as if I needed yet another reason to leave this horrible place. As soon as I heard the neighbor pass out in his room, I ran upstairs to get my landlord's granddaughter. My landlord just happened to be in Mexico on vacation. The granddaughter didn't know what to do, but I said it didn't matter because I was leaving.

I had a presentation to give at a local college fair/convention in the next hour. It was something planned for weeks, and important to my boss and coworker. I decided I would leave after finishing the conference rather than before, since I was leading one of the presentations. I put all of my good stuff in a big duffle bag, knowing that this was all I could pack for the time being. I left the house, and Hassan, and went to the convention. I put myself into work mode, and gave the presentation without a glitch.

When the convention was over and the audience filtered out, the only ones left were myself, my coworker (who was back from her Vermont trip with a freshly broken leg from skiing), and my boss. I began to exhale now that the pressure and responsibility of the presentation were gone. This gave room for the emotions I had been forcing down from all the trauma of Hassan. I started to break emotionally, and began sobbing in hysteria. I lost all control of my deep emotions. As the flood of tears fell, I began having a hard time breathing. I managed to call my mom to tell her that I was coming home now.

My boss and coworker saw my messy melt down. Out of concern, they coaxed me into walking to my boss' car in order to go see a crisis counselor. My boss kept speaking to me in soft but firm tones, saying that I needed to get help right away. I was so distraught, and they spoke with such concern, that I believed they must have been right even though I had no ability to make any kind of judgment call as to how I was currently doing. As we got into her car, Hassan called my cell phone. I answered the phone without thinking, because in that moment I could not think of anything beyond the fact that ringing phones need to be answered.

He said he had something extremely important to tell me. Panic set in. The idea that he had some deadly contagious disease screamed in my mind. I told my boss I had to get out of the car, but she was insisting on the crisis counselor, saying that I was too unstable to leave right now. My mind focused in on survival, and right now survival meant finding out what Hassan had to tell me. I argued with her, desperate for her to understand my awful situation without me needing to explain coherently. She said that if I got out of the car, I was fired. I didn't care, and opened the door.

I just about jumped out of my boss' moving car to go to Hassan's house. I was afraid that if I did not find out what Hassan needed to tell me, I would go through life with a ticking time bomb of a potential disease. I had been a virgin before Hassan raped me, and had no idea all that could happen with every sexually transmitted disease. I decided that I had to see him to find out what was extremely urgent—but afterwards, I would drive strait home to my parents in Louisiana, there was no doubt in my mind.

By this time it was around 7:00pm. Once I got to Hassan's, I was agitated that I had not had the presence of mind to simply have him tell me on the phone what he wanted to say rather than make me come out in person. After a short pause once he opened the door, I asked him impatiently what was so urgent. He casually looked at me and said it was nothing. All I could do was stare at him, completely confused. He said he had nothing to tell me, and that he knew I was about to leave—he had to stop me. I became irate, feeling like an animal just caught in a trap. I yelled that I was leaving. Before I could take one step, Hassan mentioned how dark it was outside.

Using rational logic, he laid out why it would not be the wise choice to leave right this moment. I ignored his argument . . . but I did realize that I actually didn't have any money for a hotel. I also remembered that my coworker had broken her leg and was not staying at her place, so I couldn't crash with her. I couldn't go back to my old room, the guy across the hall had just tried to break in. And my landlord was in Mexico.

He saw my face fall, and opportunistically suggested staying at his aunt's. With arms up in a defensive posture, he said "Just for one night, then head home". All of the adrenaline that had coursed through my body that day had taken a toll in exhaustion, and on the spot I could not think of any other option. His mom stepped out, saying that Hassan's aunt owed her a favor, and so it would really be no problem. I agreed outwardly without consenting to the idea fully in my mind. I would be driving over there, and so when the better idea came to me, I would just be a no show to her place.

Despite the excuses I gave in my mind for the terms of agreeing to this "favor", in reality I had just fallen for a classic manipulative technique. Hassan acted as if he really did have my best interests into consideration, and by the world's logic, it made sense. I Corinthians 3: 18 says, "Do not deceive yourselves. If any of you think you are wise by the standards of this age, you should become 'fools' so that you may become wise." God *always* provides for His children, no compromise necessary. Instead of trusting that He would find a safe place for me to stay despite the problems listed in front of me, I leaned on my own logic and rational thought. I assumed, again, that this snake would not bite me if I did nothing to agitate it. I had absolutely no clue what Hassan had planned.

I would no longer experience a single free night in New York City. From that moment until the day I ran away, I was treated as his sex slave, no longer free to leave his presence. I did not have a job to go back to. No one was alerted that I was missing because technically my boss had fired me, and my mom assumed I was staying in the city and working. I was in his grasp, 24/7. He told me when to eat, shower, speak, be happy, and of course I did not get any voice in what he wanted to do at night. Every day I dreamed of being home with my family, where this horrible nightmare did not exist. The sheer loss was palatable. My soul felt it.

Chapter 2

TRAPPED

Manipulation Games

Covert Phone Calls

Dead Roses

Every day felt like a game of chicken. Would I blink and die, or would he blink and I escape. He would say seemingly normal things to me but they always had a twist to them. Everything had some kind of test to it, some kind of meaning behind it to see how I would react, what my temperament was, or what my tolerance level was. The incredible frustration in this was that I could recognize what he was doing, and he knew that. How I would react to knowing he was testing me was, in and of itself, a test.

My survival instincts kicked in without me being aware of them most of the time. From answering questions in calculated ways so as not to upset him, to seeming interested in something that I knew he wanted me to be interested in for fear of making him angry, I would act in ways to survive that I normally never would. All of this was in an effort to win his game, and save my life. Looking back, I have been able to see and process through those survival reactions, and I now can recognize things that I did instinctively to stay alive. At the time it felt as if I was dancing on shards of glass; very, very carefully to not fall or get cut too badly. While I could tell that what he was doing was to manipulate me and size me up, to see how much "breaking" that he had to do, I also knew intrinsically that he would only be doing this if he posed a very real threat to me. He invested too much to not care about the outcome.

I could see this calculated investment of actions in the progression of how he treated me. At first, like breaking any wild thing, he expressed command and dominance. He was cruel in how he treated me at night, and he was able to do this without the shock factor from me because I did not know that what he was doing was in fact torture. I actually did not come to understand this fact until this year after having an extremely candid conversation with my counselor.

The next phase he went through was one of routine and his gain in confidence with the concept of breaking me. Then came the phase of pushing the limit on routine to see how much control he had. And the last phase of this progressive dominance and breaking was one of feeling completely confident that he had "won," meaning I was his to do with in any way he wished. Each phase came and went. I was able to see this progression because it manifested in what he would do to me and how he spoke to me. Being able to recognize his arrogance and progression of confidence was like watching a train wreck—while being the passenger. His cruelty extended beyond the night hours into daytime mental, emotional and spiritual manipulation.

MANIPULATION GAMES

Hassan would boast that he held some variation of mind reading power. I did not believe him, of course, but his continued assertions made me uneasy to respond in the way that I wanted to respond—roll my eyes. One evening, he told me that he would prove he had certain abilities. He took out a napkin and started writing something while covering the napkin with his free hand. When he had written two or three sentences, he looked up with a smirk. Still covering the napkin with his hand, he asked me to list a few general ideas in life that I hated and a few I loved. I did. He lifted his hand up, and showed me his napkin. He had written down what I said, plus or minus a few.

I knew the reaction he wanted . . . he wanted me to be astounded at his insights. I was more confused at what he wanted to prove to me than I was astounded that he could guess some concepts I enjoyed and loathed. It does not take supernatural abilities to study a person and recognize patterns in their reactions to deduct character trait appreciation. For me, I had a chill down my spine because he *wanted* me to believe he had special abilities. This whole exercise reeked of something evil to me. Power is the only reason I could rationally conclude as to why he wanted me to be in a position to believe he had special and unique abilities that the general public, and I, didn't have. Power. I did not want to think about what would go on in Hassan's mind if he felt he was losing his power over me.

On a different level, he would try to control everything I ate and drank. He decided to tell me I was not to have Diet Coke or any sweetener because it would harm me. The man repeatedly and intentionally abused me in multiple ways, yet cared about what I put into my body that could be harmful. I'm sure owners of cattle at slaughter houses feel the same way about their "property". He would tell me what we should eat and allow me to have something I wanted on rare occasions as if rewarding good behavior. He would tell me which words to use in conversation. He would go from zero to sixty in one second flat in anger if I said something with words he felt were too immature.

Trying to stay alive in a situation like this requires some very odd behavior. I was always trying to guess what answer or action would be the right one in order to keep him pacified enough to stay safe. If taken out of context and on their own, many of the conversations I had with Hassan would sound as if I wanted to be with him—as if I agreed with some of his warped views of the world and life. But the truth was that I constantly fought my gut reactions to correct him, to run away, to spit in his face—or punch it-, to tell him how awful he was. All for the sake of this paralyzing fear that I might misstep and unleash something so horrible in him that I would not survive it.

I believe that it was the Holy Spirit telling me, helping me, to be wise in this battle. One of the more tragic consequences in my view is the effect these life saving behaviors had on my psyche after I escaped. Good manipulation can be a hard lose-lose situation. Even when the manipulation didn't work in that I did not fall for his mind control to stay and be conquered, what I had to do to get out was haunting in the guilt and shame that I felt. It has taken years of counseling, all beautifully prescribed by Jesus, step by step, and trust moment by trust moment, to repair the muscle in my emotions that this guilt and shame has torn.

Using manipulation to keep me confused was always his key weapon. He had physical strength, and he did use that at various times, but I know that I could have kicked and punched him enough to cause enough damage to possibly allow my escape. My mind became part of my own stumbling. I kept trying to make sense of something purely evil that has no sense. I believe explaining the manipulation tactics used is a key part to arming against it. My prayer is that a reminder will be put in the back of your mind so that if you should see these tactics used in your life, you will not hesitate to recognize it for what it is and avoid these pitfalls.

One of his tactics was to play on my desire to have the typical relationship that every girl dreams of—a hopeless romantic who swoons every time you walk in the room, tells you everything that you want to hear about your worth and your value, and even talks about how one day he could see marriage. I wanted to be in a relationship like that. I wanted to be the girl who had the amazing boyfriend and who was so incredibly happy with where her life was going.

I imagined myself with some amazing guy having so much fun; the two of us going on cruises or hiking mountains, going to elegant dinners and fundraisers. In my fantasy, I was purely loved 100%; I wanted to be adored. This was my Achilles' heel of vulnerabilities and Hassan was able to pick right up on that. Perhaps he used part of what he knew from my past regarding my relationship with my parents and the troubles that we had had, perhaps he picked up on how I responded to him when he complimented me, perhaps there is a neon sign flashing above my head saying "love wanted", who knows. Regardless, this was one of the things that allowed his talons to get hooked deeply into me.

As part of his manipulation, he started to use the promise of an engagement ring. We actually walked into a Tiffany's one day and he told me to look around, and see what caught my eye. He said he wanted to know what style I liked because he had a friend in the city that he was going to pay to make a ring for me.

I had seen all the chick flick movies with this type of romantic fantasy. I wanted to believe so badly that I could be just like the character with a fiancé who would shut down Tiffany's so that she could pick out anything she wanted. I have a feeling that he had seen those movies as well. It was a well played manipulation plan. I, of course, did not want to marry him. I actually hated him. But . . . What he did succeed in doing was stirring the pot of all of those feelings.

I wanted to know what it tasted like to be so completely adored. I wanted that in the deepest part of my heart. Strong emotions of loneliness, desire, even fear of not having companionship crept into my thoughts, adding to my already intense battle of holding onto the truth.

On a different battle front, there was a supernatural component to my time with Hassan that is difficult to explain. While what he did physically was awful and torturous, there was a sense of evil about him that directly clashed with the

Holy Spirit inside of me. This is what makes understanding the entirety of the situation even more difficult. If my experiences were easily quantifiable and definable, I believe it would be easier for me to understand what happened, and consequently easier to heal from it. But the truth is, so much of this horror was spiritual on a level beyond my understanding.

Around the first week of my time with him, Hassan and I went to a typical American diner one night to eat. While we were there, he started challenging me around things that he felt he had abilities to do that were beyond normal typical behavior. He said that he wanted to show me.

I was still in a fog—my way of coping was just to go with the flow, and so I asked him to show me. He told me to close my eyes and give him my hands. I did, and about eight seconds went by before I peeked. He looked as if he were concentrating hard on something. He suddenly jerked his hands back while skidding backwards in his chair.

He started staring at me and breathing hard. His eyes looked as if I were pointing a gun at him or threatening him with the knife. I assure you I was just sitting there, but it looked as if he were deathly afraid of me. He also had a look of complete contempt for me. Contempt to the point of hatred. He looked disgusted. Hassan collected himself after this went on for a bit, and he told me that he had seen my body get into a horrible accident. He saw me mangled and bleeding, and told me that if I were not careful, this is what my future held.

Try to imagine my reaction. Put yourself in that situation, sitting across the table from someone you really hate but also fear. You hear this man you hate say he has superpowers and pretends to be a psychic; all while you are recognizing the manipulation and the fear tactic he is using. How dumb did he think I was? I wanted to laugh in his face, I wanted to punch his face, and I wanted to run away all at the same time. What ended up happening was a revelation from the Holy Spirit.

As soon as I saw the hate and fear combination in his eyes staring me down, I knew that this was more than a man who wanted to control me, own me, make me his sex slave or sell me overseas. This was more than my naivety getting me into serious trouble. This was more than Satan trying to tempt me. This was a full on spiritual war. He had hate and total fear of God in me! Perhaps his evil had yet to pick up fully on the Power of the Holy Spirit inside my soul before this moment. Perhaps his channeling type behavior at that table was for some type of spiritual sizing-up. Perhaps he did not know I belong to Jesus Christ. I was allowed to see something much bigger than I have ever experienced in that moment.

Somehow in the course of seconds, it all became known to me that I was in a battle; and I realized in that moment that I was very much ill equipped to be there. In my mind's eye, I looked around and saw landmines everywhere. One false move and I might trigger an explosion, to my detriment. In a matter of seconds the Holy Spirit spoke to me and I spoke back; we had a conversation and an understanding about what was going on.

I completely yielded 100% to Christ fighting this battle for me. I realized how ridiculously unarmed I was. I felt like a child lost in the woods during an insurgent attack. I climbed into Jesus' arms, and I let him have full complete control over how I was to get out of this war. From that moment until the day that I left New York, I left the battle tactics up to God while I accepted with exceeding thankfulness that I was only to hold on for the ride, knowing He wouldn't let me drop no matter how fast or bumpy the fight would become.

And the fight did become bumpy. One night, I got lost in my introspective mind, talking to God as my only friend. I was trying to process the fact that I was in this room, on this air mattress, next to this horrible person. It was cold, colorless, and silent. I began to wonder about the spiritual battle going on around me. It struck me that Hassan himself was part of the spiritual battle. So naturally, I decided to test it. I remembered a wonderful teacher I had in grade school who taught us that the concept of the blood of Jesus Christ was something demons could not stand. She had told us that if we were ever afraid, we should sing the old hymn *"What can wash away my sins? Nothing but the blood of Jesus."*

I turned to look at Hassan, and like every other night, he was awake. I never actually saw him sleep, ever. He asked me why I was looking at him. I said "Hassan, what do you think of when I say the words 'the blood of Jesus Christ'?" I stared at him slightly afraid, but fear was outweighed with boldness from the Truth. He said very quietly something I could barely make out, it sounded like "that someone would love so much." It was quiet again for a second . . . then a gasp for air came out of Hassan's mouth.

He literally threw his head backwards, and a deep guttural gasp for air came again. Then, silence. My eyes widened as much as possible. I actually had the thought that I had killed the man race through my mind. I poked his arm, but nothing. Then about three seconds later, he began breathing normally again. I could do nothing but stare at him with huge eyes and an open mouth. He looked over at me, and asked why I was staring at him like that. I said, "What just happened?!" He looked at me like I was the crazy one and said "Rachel I have no idea what you are talking about." I rolled to my other side and began dissociating out of fear as he told me to go to sleep.

I have often swung back and forth in analyzing what happened that night. I have run the gambit between his physical 'freak out' for lack of any accurate term, and his statement at the beginning concerning the love of God. All I can conclude with confidence is that God knows the truth of what controlled Hassan, and I am protected by God regardless. I also know that it had a lasting impression on me. After this night, the scales in my mind, always assessing what would be the safest response with the least amount of concession, tipped much farther to the side of stay safe. The earnestness of my desire to get out of New York City became overwhelming.

Every single morning that I woke up in New York, I wanted to be home. Before I would open my eyes, the let down of being in this situation would set in. In tension to this desire for home, I was committed to yielding to the very sensitive timing of the Holy Spirit. I did not want to make a move without His say so. This time became a continual longing prayer for endurance. Slowly, a strange form of life began to occur. Hassan and I would go to dinner, we would go to the convenience store, we even did laundry at a laundromat one time. He was careful not to make it torture all the time . . . that would be too hard of a sell for the lies he was offering me during this grooming time of will-breaking.

Rather than the 'shock into submission' 24/7 approach to his torture, he took it slow and steady—constantly toeing the line, hoping I would become entranced enough to willingly change my definition of what was acceptable. I had glimpses of things that seemed very off, but weren't so bad as to be something to make the risk of the run worth it at the consequence if my life; all while still *acting* as if I were falling for his trance. One example of this toeing the line of defining acceptable was locking my stuff in his office basement closet. I never had the intention to stay, so I had left my stuff in my car after the conference. It could of course get stolen if left in my car, and I needed things, so I brought it into his office. He brought it down to the basement and locked it up with a key he kept.

Warning bells were ringing, but only enough to stare, eye's wide like a deer who sees their predator. Until the predator moves, the deer stands perfectly still. There was a slight sense of logic that I could somewhat understand to locking my stuff in his office basement closet—his office was in fact in a dangerous neighborhood . . . and I was too tired to combat it through thinking. So, I went along with it at first.

A week into my time with him, he said that he was going to run a fast errand. This is one of the few times he ever let me out of his sight, though he left another person in the office watching me. I asked him if I could have the key for the closet in case I needed something from my bag. He said no, I was not allowed to have it. I asked why, I clearly might want something from my bag. He said *"If I give it to you, you might run away.* No."

I was watching him cross the line right in front of me. There wasn't even an attempt at subterfuge, but the line had been pushed so far back at this point, it wasn't much of a leap to cross that line and declare his intentions outright. The effect of this constant pushing of the normal, farther and farther, left me without enough room to make the running start I needed to give a reasonable objection. Up until this point, since the morning after that first night, it had been communicated through his actions rather than his words that he considered me his to own; now we had crossed into a place more dangerous, more demanding in his requirements. The less concerned he was about my potential objections to him, the more dangerous things were for me exponentially.

At this point my brain had three options. The first one was to recognize the reality of the situation, and fight against it with any consequences that might come, no matter how dangerous. The second was to recognize the reality of the situation, and simply concede to it with any consequences that might come, though perhaps saving my life. The third, and one that I subconsciously did to survive, was to pretend reality wasn't reality, and this was a fake life, a fake world. We were playing house.

This way of thinking led to very strange juxtapositions and situations. I would pretend it was normal for us to go out to eat like normal people, meet one of his friends at a bodega like normal people, obey traffic signals like normal people. At the same time, I would overhear conversations about offshore accounts in the Cayman Islands with those "friends" we met in those bodegas. Nothing could alarm me, because if it did, that would mean I was in reality and would have to make one of the other two decisions. So instead, I would flag thoughts for later processing, but continue to act as if I knew God would always be with me and that I could always talk to Him in my mind if I needed companionship. This made the pretending that life was not real all the more bearable, because I was tethered to a rock so as not to get lost in my own fantasy world. I had the "hope as an anchor for the soul" as it says in Hebrews.

Because Hassan would not let me have conversations that were not observed or overheard by him, I didn't have them. Living in isolation from any friends or family is a horrible way to experience life. I only had God, and in the most tender way possible, God communicated with my Spirit directly so that I was never alone while I was with Hassan. While I spoke to God most of every day, I still had longing for physical and kind interaction with other human beings. I remember going to Dunkin Donuts with Hassan one morning. There were so many people in the lines . . . in front of me, behind me, and on both sides of me.

Dozens of people, and no one I could talk to. I began to wonder if they had any idea that I was this man's sex slave. I did not wish my torture on any of them. I began to wonder: Were *these* people happy? Did they have friends, a spouse, even a child they were going to hug and see today? Would they cry with me if I spilled everything my heart was keeping locked in silence? If I were able to know the words in the dictionary to use that would adequately explain what this horrible man standing next to me had done, would they not forcibly restrain him while getting the police right here in Dunkin Donuts?

I wondered if there would be a kind human being that would look into my eyes and instinctively know that I needed help. I wanted rescuing so much that I could not consider really wishing for it to come at any particular time . . . my heart could not take that level of hope for freedom if it would not 100% happen right then. I knew God would get me out at some point, even if no one could see the danger and pain I was in at that moment. I had to tell myself to keep a stiff upper lip many times in the survival game. I had to tell myself to not give up or cave into total depression and hopelessness, no matter if it took one more day or one more year to get out. I continuously asked God for renewal of my mind in order to not get lulled into forgetting that His rescue would come.

I had so many conversations with God, that I began to make my own version of short-hand thoughts with Him. In the middle of the night with Hassan lying next to me, in the day with Hassan sitting next to me, in any store with multiple amounts of people next to me, it was still only me and God having any kind of meaningful communication. I believe with all my heart that this is what helped me stay sane, and keep it together long enough to not jump the gun on the Holy Spirit's timing for a safe escape. Though the fire needed to forge this precious jewel of camaraderie with my Savior was scalding hot, it was priceless in value to me.

COVERT PHONE CALLS

To help alleviate suspicion of my family, Hassan would dial my mother's cell phone number and hand it over to me, instructing me to tell my mom how happy I was, and how great everything was going. Hassan didn't have to explain what he was doing when he dialed my mom's number; he did not have to threaten me with warnings as what might happen if I misspoke. Like all of his other manipulation tactics, I behaved exactly as he wanted me to.

Looking back, I have no idea what the extent of his resources for inflicting consequences actually were, should I have not obliged his demands. That is what makes healing from situations like this so incredibly painful. It's all a game of "what if?", and how could I chance it? One day in casual conversation he looked at me and he asked how I was doing, and then quoted my Social Security number. It took me a second to realize what the numbers meant, having them said just out of the blue; but once I realized that it was my Social Security number, a new fear went all the way through me. I knew the only reason that he would be quoting it back to me, memorized, was for a threat.

I looked at him in shock, and he smiled and asked how the family was doing in Louisiana, and then quoted all of their addresses. Everything around me froze. This threat to my family wasn't even veiled. I started to panic. What had I done in meeting this man?! Had I just brought ruin to my whole family, so quickly in my life? Did my first real world experience's mistake really equal the one that would completely undo me? My family? The stress of this fear was overbearing. I hated him.

This felt like check and mate, because what would I *not* do for him in order to keep my family safe? All this manipulation and he did not have to ever show me a weapon, or tell me in detail what would happen if I didn't comply. I started wondering if I were crazy. I started questioning how, if, this were really happening. The Holy Spirit never let me lose a grip on what felt to me like indefinable truth. I trusted that God knew the truth, through all the lies, deceit, manipulation, intimidation, abuse, threats . . . through the brain-washing I had God, and God had the truth, so I knew I would somehow be okay.

In the face of such a strong warning from Hassan, I continued to do my best to keep him appeased. I re-engaged in the façade that it was more than tolerable to be with him.

Psychological manipulation is a very powerful weapon. It is also a weapon that takes dedication to use in any devastating form due to the need for repetition by the one who wants to cause permanent harm. Hassan was in this for the long run. I was not a one-time fantasy that he saw and had to have. He methodically broke me down—psychologically, emotionally, physically, sexually, even spiritually. He was breaking me like you would break a wild horse. He was trying to break my spirit.

What he didn't count on was the power of the God. Looking back, it seems like insanity would have been so close with the level of manipulation and exhaustion I was enduring. The sleep deprivation, constant monitoring my every move, no other interaction, isolation. While I would lie out of my mouth to Hassan to keep him happy and to not make waves, I would follow that lie mentally with the opposite truth so that I would not get confused beyond recovery.

In the middle of all of this manipulation and control, I was able to sneak out two phone calls. The first one was to a friend of mine back in college. She was a sorority pledge sister and one of my best friends. She knew something was very wrong because I hadn't been communicating with her. She was worried about me in a way I had never seen in her. I came to find out later that she had had the whole sorority praying for me and told the whole sorority in our weekly meetings that something was very wrong.

I snuck this call to her when Hassan had to leave the apartment to take care of something. He left his aunt in the living room, so I could not escape, but I knew if I spoke softly enough I could get a call out without her hearing. When my friend picked up the phone, she exclaimed my name and kept saying "Oh my gosh! Oh my gosh! How are you?!" I told her how much I wanted to get out of the situation so desperately. She encouraged me and cheered me on to leave. We even made plans for spring break to go to the beach in Florida.

I knew the likelihood of my being able to fulfill a plan for a spring break vacation was almost non-existent. But for that moment, making plans with her made me feel like I was free— like the person who has been given two months to live yet plans next year's Christmas season. I had to give myself that moment, even if it was impossible to fulfill. The call only lasted about three minutes, but gave me about three days worth of extra hope in my tank that I could endure this.

The second call was to my mom. It was in the middle of my time with Hassan. I was taking out the dirty mop water and dumping it in the back alley. While I was outside, I shut the door to the back entrance of his workplace and snuck a call to my mom. It lasted for only one minute, but that was enough. All I had time to tell her was how much I hated it here and that I was coming home.

She was so excited, I could hear it in her voice. She kept saying "praise God, praise God, praise God". I told her I would get back in touch with her soon. I wasn't able to make a call after that, there were no other times that I was left alone long enough to make any kind of call. A few days after this covert call to my mom, Hassan and I were leaving a restaurant when he told me to get out my phone. I did, and he dialed my mom's number for me in order to have one of our arranged conversations about how well my life was going here in New York.

When she saw my number and answered, she was so excited to hear my voice. The first thing out of her mouth was asking when I was leaving to come back home. Hassan was sitting right next to me, so I had to sell that I was happy where I was, and that I was not going anywhere. I could feel Hassan's stare on my face. I felt like a child who was caught doing something disobedient. I spoke to my mom in a way to appease Hassan without any room for doubt. I said to my mom, "What do you mean? This is my home now." She was silent except for a quiet, almost whisper, of "What?" I repeated that this was my home now and that she needed to understand that. I know hearing me say those horrible words broke her heart completely. I can only imagine what she could have been feeling at that moment, and I hate that she went through that.

DEAD ROSES

The days went by like this, slowly and methodically. My goal was simply to get through any current day. I did not have the energy to focus on anything other than breathing and existing. I was worn down beyond what I thought I ever would have been able to take. I was also exhausted. Yet somehow, my body kept moving when I told it to. I began to get emotional out of the stress I was going through. Perhaps Hassan picked up on this, perhaps he wanted to keep working some angle on me, I'm really not certain; but one day while we were driving around, he bought some long stem roses from someone selling them on the side of the road.

He was giving a ride to a friend, so it was the three of us in my car. He turned to the friend and, while in front of me, said that I needed appeasing because "you don't want your woman mad." In a very twisted way I actually had to ask God to remind me that I was not the cause of his discomfort. I hadn't done anything wrong to Hassan by being angry and exhausted. That I was even thinking this way in that moment is absurd and shows how I was holding on by my fingertips.

I also had to remember that it was his manipulation to try to equate being unenthusiastic with what he called being mad.

Despite the valid frustration at his statement, the last thing I wanted to do was make him angry. And now he had made it clear that he saw it as my fault for being depressed about the situation, and equated it in his mind with my being angry at him. This forced me to be all the more of an actress in going along with things.

Maybe it was just the adrenaline that was added to the situation by knowing he now wanted my attitude in addition to actions, but I found the energy to behave both in action and attitude. Back at the place where we were staying, I put the roses in a cup on the windowsill. I thought that maybe I could imagine myself in some sort of beauty. Perhaps if I had a flower next to me I could convince myself that things were not so terrifying.

What I found, though, was that they did not cheer me. In fact, the opposite was true. Seeing the flowers alive and blooming made me jealous and very unsettled. I wanted to bloom! I wanted to be beautiful. I wanted to feel and be alive. Time went on, and I forgot about the roses. They eventually died, but I left them on that windowsill anyway. Towards the end of my capture with Hassan, there was one particular night where I woke up from this dissociation fog I had been living in.

He was on top of me like every other night, but all of the sudden I realized how depraved his acts were, right then in that moment. Everything started to look so ugly in my world. Everything felt wrong and backwards. I started to get overwhelmed at the vulgarity and decided to give one more push of resistance. I put my hands under his chest and tried to bench press him off of me. He pinned me down and maneuvered in a way to where I couldn't move. He then said, "Just take what I'm giving you." A piece of me died that moment in my heart. I remember being shocked that all I was able to muster in an attempt to put an end to this was so easily squashed. I wasn't dissociating anymore, I wasn't in a fog, I was not in a dream anymore.

I was keenly aware of what he was doing and that my efforts to get free had failed. I turned my head to look out the window and I saw the dead roses on the windowsill. At that moment, I gave up. I hit a turning point, from the place of playing coy at his game to stay alive until I could leave, to a place of having my lively spirit broken like a horse. I had tried so hard to keep a piece of sanity, to keep a piece of the real me alive until I could escape.

But I was so tired of the mental game. I was incredibly tired from physical lack of sleep. I was tired of feeling terrified, tired of walking on glass eggshells, and now I felt defeated to my core. A mothering compassion came over me regarding my dead flowers. I only wanted to reassure them now. I became almost peaceful in accepting that I was dying inside, as if the dead roses and I belonged together. The dead roses understood me. We were both once vibrant in life, such potential to bloom into enormous beauty. But we were cut off and isolated instead. With him still on top of me, I decided to escape into a dream world purposefully. I couldn't handle being in this real world anymore.

I escaped in my mind, back to my days in college with my friends. I pretended that I was back in school where the only thing I worried about was finishing an assignment on time. I thought about the cafeteria and how fun it was to be able to eat with friends for every meal. I dreamt of how independent I was in college, able to make any choice I wanted that, now, were luxuries. Choices like when and what to eat, when to sleep, who to call and with whom I could speak. I dreamt of my sorority's dance performance for the school competition . . . and decided to stay in that memory.

I don't remember the details of the last few weeks of my time in New York after that night. Somehow they went by with me barely existing. Every day came without any spark or any kind of personality to make it unique. I did what I was told without any significant independent thought. Eventually all of this wearing down physically and mentally caused my emotions to catch up with me . . . I began breaking down into tears multiple times a day. Out of sheer exhaustion I could not force myself to stop crying. Hassan was very annoyed, so he decided one afternoon to open the door to the place where we were staying and said, "If you want to leave then go right now. I dare you to get up and walk out of here now."

I wanted nothing more than to run, and let all of Hassan's world implode upon itself with every step away from him I took—but somehow I couldn't make myself get up. He was holding the door open, and I was on the floor sobbing on all fours, unable to get up and leave. I am not exactly sure what I was afraid of; I don't know if deep down I knew that he was bluffing and would actually take some sort of retaliation. Perhaps I had been whipped so much that I became like one of those elephants who is chained by one leg for so long that any hope the chain will ever be removed is forgotten.

When the elephant's chain is actually removed, the elephant never tries to leave. I was split in two mentally . . . if I ran outside, would the sunshine capture me and give me enough reassuring warmth that I could remember I am valued deeply in this world? I carried so much shame within me at that time, in addition to the emotional and physical pain. Could I make it through this pain and be happy, or was it all futile at this point? Would there be kindness in strangers, or was I really as naive as Hassan said I was? Did the wonder of warmth and kindness even exist anymore? I stayed on the floor crying rather than running out.

I could not make myself take the chance of having one more blow to any hope that had been raised. I wasn't willing to chance that the world outside this dark room with Hassan would not be able to gather me up with enough protection to be okay. I sat on the floor in panic and desperation. Hassan's words from the first week resonated in my mind. He had said "I know you Rachel. You won't ever leave, because you can't take the fact that the person you will eventually marry will not be the only person you will have had sex with." I did not believe him on the surface. On a deep level, however, part of me could not let that concept go. I was so wrapped up in shame that I could not see clearly. The truth is that God will forgive All sins.

I also had not made this choice—Hassan himself had admitted to raping me. All of this was beyond my understanding while sitting on that floor. I slumped over, depressed at the reality of my life at that moment and despondent that I could not get up and walk out. The Holy Spirit did not let me sit there without feeling His truth, however. I still, even after this paralysis moment, was resolute that God would absolutely get me out of here as soon as it was safe.

Sure enough, shortly after this I got sick and developed a urinary tract infection. I remember it preventing me from tolerating sex all together . . . this was probably the one thing that was unacceptable to Hassan. With this as his motivation, we went to a walk-in ER clinic.

Chapter 3

MY ESCAPE

The ER

Almost Saudi Arabia

A Camry-Shaped Angel

THE ER

Because Hassan was not a family member, he was not able to go back into the exam room with me. This was one of the first miracles that I could recognize in the very moment it was occurring. I remember breathing a huge sigh of relief that I would be out of his ever watching eye. The doctor asked a lot of questions, and I listed off my physical complaints. One of my complaints was lower back pain that I had not ever felt before.

She looked at me curiously and asked about my sexual activity. I could feel myself turning red. It dawned on me that I might be pregnant . . . I quickly did the calculation in my mind and realized I was overdue for my cycle. I asked her to run a pregnancy test. While I was waiting for the results, I remember praying over and over "Please God, do not let me be pregnant, please God, please God." I was afraid of being tethered to Hassan legally forever. I thought about the idea of running away and never telling him, but what if he found me? He had memorized my social security number, what if he sued me for rights? I sat waiting, feeling sick with the possibilities.

The doctor came back and told me the test was negative. I gave a big sigh and smile. She asked me if I had ever had an exam by a gynecologist. I said no, not even sure what it all entailed. She escorted me to an adjoining room. While walking over to that room, I looked at the center of the large room housing nurse stations and testing equipment. This sterile and unfamiliar place made me actually feel safe. The nurses and doctor were looking out for me, for my best interests. I felt a comfort that was like a warm memory from long ago.

During the procedure, the doctor made note of the physical trauma that she observed. She spoke in great compassion, "You know that you can say no, right?" I looked at her and said that yes, I knew that. But in reality, a light bulb had just gone off in my mind. I still had the ability to say no! It was like the fog had cleared in a great blast and I saw clearly. I had been lulled into submission just like the elephant without a chain. Hassan had been letting up lately in watching me because I had fallen into his brainwashing and manipulation.

I had forgotten that this wasn't the way life had to be, and that I could in fact be free. I consider that doctor an angel. She was so kind and patient. And she gave me hope. I do not wish any girl to have her first gynecological exam to be in an ER room after enduring multiple rapes; but even in this horrible situation, God sent someone to speak truth to me along the way.

I received medicine for the infection, and some pills that allowed me to become numb while the infection healed. When I left the exam room, Hassan was waiting for me in the lobby. I looked at him with a hidden smirk because I knew something he did not—my spirit was not broken anymore. Now it was just a matter of waiting for God for safety and then running, like I had felt when I first fell into Hassan's lure.

We left in my car to go back to the apartment. As I was driving, he turned to me and he asked if I had received some pills for numbing. I said that yes, I had, and asked why? He said "because I don't care if you want it, I don't care if it hurts . . . you will be mine tonight." I looked at him in disbelief as that old feeling of cold fear came upon me. I did not say anything. My mind tried to process the kind of person that would say such a horrible thing . . . and then I realized that . . . I might *actually* die staying with him.

As soon as we got back to the apartments, I went to bed. The next day he was very watchful over me. It felt like a test, to see if either what he had said would embolden me, or if the ER trip had emboldened me. I knew I had to convince him that neither had occurred. I had to convince him of something beyond this; that I loved him and that I considered myself to be owned by him. I told him that concept the whole day in various ways. I said that there was nobody for me but him, and that I hated having to be examined at the ER because I did not want anyone to have access to me except him.

I remember rolling my eyes in my mind and laughing at him in my imagination. I was putting on an Academy level performance for him. I could see in his face that he was convinced enough. He believed me, and thought he had trumped me. He even let his guard down on one of his manipulation lies.

SAUDI ARABIA

The day after the ER trip, I could tell that he was starting to lose his grip on his own lies and manipulation. He told me that he could see how stressed I was. He said that he knew I was not ready for an engagement ring, and so he had the ring shipped to a friend of his in India to make a necklace instead. I had never told him the type of ring that I liked or any other specific that he had said he was waiting for in order to have his friend here make the ring in the first place.

There was no ring. I did not let him know that I realized his lie, of course. Instead I smiled, and said thank you; but inwardly I was praising God that I was able to catch him in a lie like this. It was important to me to be able to see as much truth as I could, and catching him in this lie just added fuel to my truth fire.

In addition to this surprise necklace, he also had a trip that he wanted us to go on. He said that he wanted to take me to Saudi Arabia. As I pretended to be excited, I knew there would never be any way I would get on a plane with him. I played coy and said "oh wow, how fun. Why Saudi Arabia?" Hassan told me it was an amazing place, a special place, and he wanted to share it with me. He said it was really important to him for me to go with him specifically to Saudi Arabia. I knew in a nanosecond what he was really trying to do.

When I was in high school, my government and ethics teacher my senior year showed us the video Not Without My Daughter. In that movie, a woman trusts her husband and goes to Iran with him and their daughter. While there, her husband decides that they are going to live permanently in Iran, and does not let his wife leave. She has to dangerously escape Iran, and does so with their daughter. There was no way on this earth that I would ever leave American soil willingly with Hassan. I praised God at that very moment for my high school senior government teacher.

What I did not know then, was that Saudi Arabia is a country were men in the sex trade particularly like white women. A good friend of mine who is in the law enforcement field on the Federal level helped me through the process of turning Hassan into the FBI. As my friend and I were walking through the details, I asked if there is any significance to Saudi Arabia. He said the most preferred type of woman to own in Saudi is a white woman. This made so much sense to me, like seeing how some of this puzzle fit together. Hassan was not from Saudi Arabia, did not speak their language, and was not of their religion. What was Saudi Arabia to Hassan? Having my friend explain this preference made sense, gave me a feeling of validity in my suspicions, and had made me fall to my knees in grief and gratitude.

I did not have to keep up the pretense of deciding to go to Saudi Arabia with Hassan for very long. The next morning, two days after the visit to the ER, Hassan let me open his office alone for the first time. I think he believed I really was convinced of his lies, and did not pose a threat to run away. He said was tired He said he was tired and that he wanted to sleep in. As soon as I woke up and realized this, I knew that it was my moment to **run**. I knew I could not look suspicious . . . I did not get my bag, any of my clothes, or any of my other belongings. I was sure to wear my lucky sweatshirt that morning, not wanting to leave it behind. I got my keys and told Hassan I would see him in a few hours at the office.

I never went to his office that morning. I got in my car and started driving without looking back. I wanted to drive as far as I could without stopping, and so right outside of the city I decided to fill the car up with gas. I had a feeling of hope again! I was almost free. I wanted to get a full tank, get a cup of coffee, and watch all of New York in my rearview mirror. After filling up and paying for the gas and coffee, I got in my car and settled in for a long drive. I turned the key in the ignition, and . . . nothing. I shook it off and turned the key again, but still nothing. It gave a grinding whine rather than the sound of a roaring engine. I took a breath and went inside to ask for help. The gas station attendant looked outside and asked "why did you put diesel in your car"?

I was really confused. Not knowing anything about cars, I asked if that is a bad thing, or if it would still drive. Before I let him answer I blurted out "Because I really need it to be fixed as soon as possible, I have to get on the road." The gas station attendant looked at me as if I was an idiot, and said "your car is not going to go anywhere, you. put. diesel. in. it." He said the last words with extra pronunciation. I started to panic. I looked at the man in line behind me, and I started to tear up quickly. I wanted to explain to this gas station attendant that I was *running away!* and that I was quickly running out of time to actually make it! I wanted to explain to him that a very bad man might find me . . . I needed to leave now. Instead, the Lord gave me an idea and the words to say to him.

A CAMRY-SHAPED ANGEL

I asked him if I could push my car to the side of the gas station, which happened to be out of view from the highway. He said he had no problem with that so long as I would have someone come to tow it to a repair shop. I nodded, and then called my mom. I asked her to book a plane ticket for me in my name. She was in a meeting, but as soon as she found out that it was me calling, she stopped her meeting immediately and took my call. I could hear her on the other end of the line telling the people in her meeting that "It's my daughter! It's her!" She booked the next flight that she could, giving me the confirmation number and her credit card number in case I had any trouble. I then called cab to take me from the gas station outside of New York City to the airport. While waiting for the cab, I pushed the car to the side of the gas station with the attendant's help.

I talked to my mom on the phone the whole cab ride to the airport, and I have never heard her so relieved on a phone call. She kept asking if this was really going to happen, and I kept telling her yes, I am going to the airport right now. As soon as I got to the airport, I went straight to the flight terminal and sat in the waiting room to leave. I turned my phone off. I still had some time before the flight, but I knew that Hassan might try to call, and I was afraid of even his number coming on my phone. I wanted absolutely nothing to do with him.

The airplane took off and landed. I had made it home. I was in shock . . . I was free. I turned my phone back on once we landed, and realized I had multiple voice messages. And, I realized that God had performed a miracle for me while I was flying home.

I listen to my voice messages, and heard many from Hassan. Most of them were threats to find me and take me back. Some of them were lamenting at how sad he was that I was not with him. But one of the messages made my hair stand on edge. In the message, Hassan told me that he drove to my old place in New York once he realized I had run from him. He said that he saw my car outside of my old place, and that because he knew I was inside, he decided he would let me sit in the house. He felt I could use some time to think about what I had done. He stopped looking for me when he saw my car outside the house, because why continue? He knew where I was. Except, me and my car were no where near that house.

At the time of this message, I was in the middle of a flight halfway across America. My car was 40 miles south of the city, stuck outside some gas station. Hassan, the man who had memorized my license plate, social security number, and family's address was convinced that my car was outside of my old place in New York City. There is only one explanation to me. I believe God had an Angel get into the form of a Toyota Camry so that Hassan would not come looking for me. What a Father we have! There are so many miracles that God has done, so many unexplainable events. My escape was a miracle. And, once I had escaped, I began the very long journey of healing. In Psalms 147:3 it says, "God heals the brokenhearted, and binds up their wounds."

Chapter 4

MY HEALING

Sex Slavery Patterns
Freedom Under a Desk
Colorado

SEX SLAVERY PATTERNS

I was nervous on the flight coming home. I didn't know what would be different and what would be the same in an always home-feeling kind of way. Getting into my mom's car felt strange. It looked and smelled the same as her car had always looked and smelled, but it felt very different. On the way home, my mom said that we needed to stop at the store to grab a few things. She pulled into the parking lot of Wal-Mart.

I had just escaped sexual slavery, and now, a few hours later, I was with my mom at a Wal-Mart. Is it really that easy to go back to normal life? Is this the new normal that I wanted? As we were shopping, she broached the subject, saying that she had been really worried about me. She went on to say that had I been gone one more week, my two brothers and uncles were going to fly to New York to get me. She had hired a private investigator to follow me around because she was so worried about me. I stared at my mom with my mouth hanging open; I had no idea that I was being followed while I was in New York.

She told me that the private investigator had started a few weeks ago with following Hassan and I around. The private investigator reported back to my mom just a few days before this day that I came home. He told my mom that she needed to get all the men that she could in my family, or any men that we knew as family friends, and, with enough guns for each, go up to New York to physically get me out. The private investigator told my mom that because I was an adult, he couldn't just capture me and take me, or else he would. The activities that he observed Hassan and I doing were a common pattern when a girl is about to get sold overseas. He said that he had seen a lot of these patterns specifically from foreign men who are from the same country as Hassan, and who had financial dealings in the Caribbean or Cayman Islands.

Mom looked at me straight in the face and told me that this private investigator said, "In my opinion ma'am, your daughter is about to be sold overseas, and if that happens, you will probably never see her again."

The hazy picture started to become clear in my mind. Every single previous conversation with Hassan, every lie, every manipulation, every conversation that I overheard—all of it started to fall into place and make sense with this insight. Saudi Arabia . . . why such an interest? All of the brainwashing, all of the breaking down of my spirit, all of the sexual abuse, guarding me 24/7. All the conversations about Cayman Island accounts. It all crashed into me in a shockingly horrible way.

Had I really been *that* close? Had I almost been a life snuffed out, never to be heard from again?

As I recall all of this now, I am brought to tears. There is nothing that separates me from <u>any</u> <u>other</u> <u>girl</u> that gets stuck in any foreign country, being viciously sold into sex slavery, other than divine intervention. Nothing but the grace of God. This is difficult to accept at times. As is His grace from the Cross to save us from the death of our sins. Grace by definition is unearned. I did nothing in and of myself to end up free today. Every girl who is still sold in slavery has just as much grace from Jesus Christ as I have; His sovereign plan is mysteriously different in how we see that grace manifested on Earth.

I know that God's plan for intervention for me was in part so that I could spread this testimony to others and warn girls to run from men like Hassan. The miracles that God did in order to get me out are not taken lightly by me; I do not take any one of them for granted. I feel that God has given me a divine instruction to share what happened, what almost happened, and how God moved in Heaven and on Earth in order to get me out. Back when being told all of this in the Wal-Mart, I couldn't fully understand or appreciate the magnitude of what I had been told. I was too traumatized. I nodded and told my mom that I loved her. I don't think either of us at that time could understand or comprehend what it meant . . . so we just went about our shopping at Wal-Mart.

The next day, I went back to see my friends in college. I went to a sorority meeting, thanking them for praying for me. I slept on different friends couches, and even visited my old workplace. It was a little surreal to have gone from something so horrible back to the world that I had known before for my first experience on my own. I stayed at my old college for about a week and then went back to my parents house. When I got back home the questions about my future started. "What are your plans?" became a common question in our household.

FREEDOM UNDER A DESK

I honestly had no idea. Do I go to work until I can get into grad school? I had already missed the deadline for applications for the coming fall. Do I try to find a job in my bachelors degree? Would that mean I had to continue living with my parents? My mom suggested offhandedly that I look into a program at Focus on the Family. It sounded a little hokey to me, but I told her I would look into it.

The program at the Focus on the Family Institute actually seem to be quite interesting once I looked into it. It was a combination program of intellectual classes on religion and society, as well as a program of personal growth with a small group of accountability partners, all set in the scene of the Rocky Mountains in Colorado Springs. It was a semester long program and I would be applying to attend in the fall.

The deadline for application was 10 days away. They required essays, personal references from friends and professors, even previous employer information. I decided to give it a shot. I borrowed my grandmother's car again, mine was still in New York, and drove back to the college campus. I found friends and professors, and was able to get every requirement that I needed in order to apply to the Focus on the Family Institute.

Once I got back home, I sent the application via overnight with two days to spare.

I knew I would not hear back on my acceptance into the program for a few weeks, so the question still remained . . . what I would do in the meantime? The first thing that I needed to do was to let go of trauma and crisis mode. I began seeing a counselor on a weekly basis. At first I also looked for work, something to fill my time. As the days went by, I stopped living off pure adrenaline and my body became very sick. Looking back, I realize this time was the first of a process of healing time for me.

I was able to sleep as much as I needed, and having been diagnosed with mononucleosis, sleep was the best thing I could do for myself. I would go to counseling once a week, go to church on Sundays with my parents, go to the library once a day to check my email and play online for half an hour, and the rest of the time I would sleep. After about a month and half, I got a call from Focus on the Family.

They told me that I had been accepted into the program! This was wonderful news . . . as much as I absolutely love my parents, I was not made to live with them as an adult. We were already clashing in many ways. I appreciate my parents for being willing to allow me to stay in their home in Louisiana, but after experiencing what I went through in New York, it was so hard to figure out how to go back to normal life. How do you un-ring a bell of that size?

A few weeks before I left for Colorado, my counselor confronted me with the need to discuss what happened in New York. Up until this time, I had been unable to talk about it. I gave very cryptic hints as to what was going on in my heart and mind, and I would show her my journaling notebook. I was living in a functional traumatized manner. My journal was full of very dark drawings and poems. I had begun doing self injury intensely at that time in an attempt to cope with inexplicable feelings and emotions. I was so incredibly wounded that getting through a day was work enough.

Living with so much trauma caused my problems to have problems of their own. My time with the counselor up until this point had been dealing with all of those issues. It was so important to go slowly for me. She knew how constant and still she needed to stand in order for me to be able to land in my own free will. With Colorado quickly approaching, she wanted to get to the heart of what had happened. I knew she was right.

She had me journal everything that had happened so that I could bring it in and read it to her. I think I associated about five times that week while journaling. I would go off in my own world and lose time. A lot of the things I couldn't remember. Some of the things brought so much shame with the memories, it was too overbearing for the moment. I did the best I could, knowing I had a deep desire to get all of what happened off my chest. When I went to her office for our session, she asked if I was ready. I said yes, and opened my mouth to speak—but nothing would come out. I shifted in my chair, took a deep breath and tried again; but still, I could not make myself speak.

I felt exposed physically, like I couldn't control my environment while sitting in that chair, in an open room, with a door anyone could walk into, or a window anyone could see in. I started to get anxious and desperate at the same time. I really wanted to be able to get this off my chest! No matter how hard I tried though, I couldn't speak. I tried to imagine what I needed to be able to talk and the only thing that I could think of was being able to completely control everything around me.

I asked her if I could crawl under her desk. I thought that this way, I would be able to feel what was behind me feel what was to each side of me. I would have the chair to cover the front of me, and the floor underneath me. I felt a little ridiculous asking, but of course she was gracious and said yes. I went over to her desk, crawled under it, and pulled the chair in front of me so that I was encapsulated by the desk. I felt like there would be no way Hassan could pop out of hiding and get me if I spoke under that desk.

In that position, I recited for the first time everything that happened in New York with Hassan. From how we met and how I escaped, to every deviant sexual act he did to me in the in between. When I was done, it was really quiet . . . so I said in a meek voice "the end." I climbed up from under the desk and saw that my counselor was crying. I wasn't even crying. I will never forget the compassion and love that I saw in her face with her tears coming down.

The sheer amount of care that she had for me gave me more courage and hope to keep moving forward in life than anything that she had said in the entire month of counseling prior to that day. This was my last session with her, but I wasn't feeling very strong in myself. I asked her to write me a note telling me I would be okay. I needed something tangible I could reference anytime that I needed. I wanted to take some of this comfort with me to Colorado. She wonderfully did so, and I have that note still today.

COLORADO

A week later I was on a plane to Colorado Springs, Colorado. My time in Colorado was a pure miracle from God. I honestly do not know how I would have healed or re-adapted back into life had it not been for the ability to take a break—a timeout of sorts—from real life in order to decompress. What better way to decompress than around Christian friends, mentors, and the Rocky Mountains?

In addition to an amazing program, amazing friends, the Garden of the gods, and learning quite a bit about Christian worldviews and society, I slowly began to heal. At this point, healing meant being able to laugh in conversations and get into a simple routine that required me to be responsible and get up in the morning. I was also able to speak about what happened for the first time to another person other than my counselor back home. I fumbled around how to fit into normal life. I tried my best to explain when asked "what made you come to the Institute?" I even tried to be bold and use my experience to help someone. I am very glad this Body of Christ was gracious and loving when I needed extra patience to re-use my trust muscles.

Chapter 5

MY WITNESS

Speaking To The Police

Speaking Out Loud

Speaking Despite The Enemy

Ephesians 3:20

"Now to him who is able to do immeasurably more than

all we ask or imagine, according to his power

that is at work within us."

Over the next six years, God continued to do miracles in my healing from this experience. I got into grad school right after Colorado, and moved back to the South. This was a perfect scenario for me because I was not ready to live in the real world quite yet. I wanted the protection of being a student, with a student advisor telling me what my future should look like, and professors telling me how I was doing at that future. I wanted regulations and schedules to guide my everyday existence.

I knew how to be a student. I was good at studying and enjoyed learning. This allowed me also to have the pressure off regarding responsibility to take care of myself financially. I was worried that I wouldn't be able to perform at a job, since my first experience in the real world job-wise crashed in flames. I had student loans to help me through the grad school process.

Life became simple again, and that's exactly what I needed. The first semester when classes began, I found a little one bedroom apartment. I got a dog, made friends at a new church and started a small group Sunday class. After a few months, the dust started settling and I began to relax. As life started to return to normal, issues begin to surface that I had been pushing down since leaving New York City. I began to have Post-Traumatic Stress Disorder. I had a hard time functioning in everyday simple things. My behavior began to take on an extreme feel to it, always pushing limits as if I had nothing to lose. I would sob at night to God, asking for help. I would wonder if Hassan had followed me, and would pop out at any moment to take me back.

I spoke with my Sunday Bible class teacher, sharing my problems and concerns with her. We are still friends to this day. We both reminisce in awe of God at the amazing beginning of this healing journey. After listening compassionately, she suggested some counseling. She looked up the name of a counselor who worked at the counseling center at our church.

I called the counseling center's office the next day and asked about making an appointment. The receptionist at the front desk said "how about two o'clock tomorrow?" I of course said yes, a little surprised at how easy it was to get into her office. I went to the counseling appointment, and met the counselor. Once we sat down in her office to begin, the first thing she did was ask how on earth I got an appointment. She said her schedule was full and had been full for a while. She said she was not taking on new clients.

I told her that when I had called, they gave me an appointment for the next day. She raised an eyebrow and asked me to tell her about myself. I was a little disappointed to learn that she was unavailable, but decided to utilize the time God had given me. I chatted with her in generalities about my story. After I left, she followed up with me by email. She said that she knew God had directed me to her, and was so convinced this was a work of God, that she would give up her lunches one day every week for me so that we could meet.

This was a beautiful act of God. Her specialty as counselor was sexual abuse and sexual trauma. I have no doubt in my mind that God ordained my steps in meeting this person and having her be a very important piece of my healing journey.

I met with her regularly for a couple of years, which happened to be my first few years in grad school. I am certain that I would not have been able to do the level of work that we needed to do to address the level of PTSD that I had if I were not a student. I could arrange my class schedule around my counseling schedule to allow for days where I had no responsibilities, in case I had high anxiety from the PTSD resolution work. I thank God so much for that gift of healing counseling.

My time with that counselor came to an end, and I felt strong enough to try to reengage in life in a more substantial way. It was around this time that I felt I was finally able to accept that God returned my joy to me. Smiling and laughing, finding pure excitement in the community of God's people, and in God's love returned to me. The next big step in my healing process didn't come until the statute of limitations deadline for legal action against Hassan.

SPEAKING OUT TO THE POLICE

I went back to a new counselor at the same counseling center at my church to help me process this anniversary and figure out what God might be telling me to do. After a few weeks of talking, the new counselor felt God was telling her strongly that we need to alert the authorities in New York City because of the fact that his business centered around children. She felt strongly that the children might be in danger knowing his level of depraved indifference to me. I did agree with her, but this was agonizing . . . now it felt like not only did I have the trauma for myself that I had experienced to go through, I also had a higher duty to get over my own trauma for the sake of someone else.

And they were children that were at stake to top it off . . . How could I not step up for them? At the same time, how in the world could I turn Hassan in and face all of that terrorizing fear and paralyzing horror that he put me through. It was an awful place to be in to make a decision. I melted down and cried so hard in front of that sweet counselor. Gross, sobbing, snotty gasps for air. She was incredibly loving and kind to me.

She listened to everything that I sobbed about—fears of saying something so official to the authorities, fears of what he might do, fears of what that makes me, fears of it being so real that I can't ever take it back and decide to live in a fantasy again. She told me go outside into the church courtyard to collect myself and to pray for as long as I needed. She said that when I was done I could come back up and she would be waiting for me.

So I did. I went down to the courtyard and I prayed desperately for God to tell me what to do. I texted a few friends who were really close to me, including my dear friend that was my Sunday Bible class teacher. My fears and my emotions were screaming at me, saying how on earth could you ever shake this horrible hornets' nest . . . but the compassion in my heart, and womanly mother instinct screamed for protection of those kids—not to mention justice against Hassan. My decision never was completely concrete. I had doubts all throughout; but I knew that one of the mainstays of how God calls us to act is with selflessness.

And so I went back upstairs, sat down in the counselor's office, and said that I would make the call to the New York City Child protective division. Today, I am immeasurably thankful that we made that call! I had no idea the amount of relief it would bring. I had no idea how much regret I would have had if I hadn't made that call. When we called, there were still two weeks left before the statute of limitations deadline. I gave them away to get in touch with me through the counseling center using my counselor as a liaison. It was an anonymous call of course. I wanted to protect my safety, but I did want the opportunity for some sort of an investigation to be possible should the police want one.

The police never called but I knew that I had given opportunity for God to move if He had willed it, and that made all the difference to me. I am fine surrendering to the sovereignty of God; what it was that He wanted to do in that situation. What I was not okay with was the concept of shutting off the possibility from the valve by refusing to have the courage to say yes to God's request.

SPEAKING OUT LOUD TO OTHERS

The next moment in my life where God pushed healing forward came in the form of ministry a few years later. I had begun going to a program my church called <u>Celebrate Recovery</u>. It is for any hurt, hang-up, and habit that one finds in their life along the way; and is a great place of community to help parse through what God is trying to tell you. Because I'd been going regularly, I had the opportunity to give my testimony to a group of people for the first time in my life.

Prepared for what I was going to say, I decided that I wouldn't hold anything back and let God do what He wanted to do. I asked a couple of friends to come and sit in the audience. I wanted some comforting and familiar faces that had been with me in the journey from the time I moved back south until that moment. I shared what God had done in my life in New York, and what He had done since then, and I believe that He was praised and exalted that day.

I went home afterwards on a little bit of cloud nine because of the sheer accomplishment of embracing the victory that God had already set before me. I began thinking, and became curious about Hassan. I had just spoken about all of the previously inexpressible pain he had caused me. I had not cared to know anything about what happened to him up until this point . . . but I started to wonder in general what might've become of him. I decided to google him. What I found was remarkable.

I found a news story from the New York DA office stating that Hassan had been arrested the year before. He was indicted on over 40 counts of conspiracy and theft regarding the business relating to children. That business ended up being a shell company for his illegal activity. His arrest date? The exact day that I ran away. Five years earlier to the day! I screamed in joy to my Father God, who loves me so much that He would pull out His shotgun like any Southern daddy, and say "not my daughter".

I can't explain how protected and astounded I am at the beautiful gift of protection God gave me that day. Two weeks prior to the day of his arrest also happened to be the day I had called the New York City Child Protective Division with the help of my counselor and informed them about Hassan. I have no confirmation to know if my phone call made one bit of a difference in this decision to arrest Hassan for these theft and conspiracy charges . . . but it doesn't matter. Just the possibility that it might have made a difference, and knowing what my counselor and I did that day in calling, knowing I was not a victim silenced by him, is enough.

This confidence boost by God as my Father allowed the inklings of ministry to filter into my heart when it came to my testimony. A couple of months later I had the opportunity to go into prison and give my testimony. I had felt some rumblings in my spirit about what it was that God was wanting me to do. I was feeling the urge to share, and the urge to be called to give the miracles of what He had done for me without reserve. I accepted God's challenge. I did not know how to go about sharing my testimony in this type of capacity, but I trusted Him to tell me as I would be looking for it.

SPEAKING OUT DESPITE THE ENEMY

A week before I was set to speak in the prison, my jaw locked shut. I had been having TMJ issues prior to this date, but it had only shut a couple of times on me since I was fifteen. To shut at this point was very frustrating. I began to wonder if I would be able to actually speak at the prison, but decided to keep the date scheduled. I trusted that God would do something, even if it meant I could not speak. My jaw remained shut up until the day I had to go into the prison and speak. It was pushed so close to time that I even had a friend offer to read what I had written for me in case I could not get it open while I was there. I ended up being fine, and was able to speak God's miracles. Praise the Lord, three women came to know Christ that day in prison.

A couple of months later, God gave me the opportunity to speak at a few churches around town. I set the dates to speak a few months out from when I receive the invitation, because my foot at the time was broken. When the dates to speak were getting closer, my foot would not show progress in healing. I was looking at needing bone graft surgery in order to aid in the healing. I wasn't certain that I would have the energy to hobble my way up to the podium to speak each night. Despite the broken foot, I was able to go and share my testimony at each of the five churches.

A couple months later, God gave me the inspiration, and strong instruction, to write this book. I had wrestled with it for a while. I wasn't sure that it was all that appropriate to share, but I wanted to be obedient. God whisper-screamed in the most gentle way possible through the Holy Spirit for me to listen to Him. It became to my spirit that not doing this book was not an option. So I began to type. One week after I began the typing for this book, I developed extreme pain in my right elbow. I noticed my right hand had pain as well. The pain showed up in my left elbow and wrist too the next week. I was in enough pain to where I could not type any more. I made an appointment with a rheumatologist to see what was happening. I was diagnosed that day with rheumatoid arthritis.

I think about all of this and I actually laugh at the attempts that Satan has done to stop me from proclaiming the word of God through this book and the miracles that He has done for me. Praise the Lord that there was always a way I have been able to share in the midst of the challenge. I told a friend of mine of the struggle of pain from typing with the rheumatoid arthritis. She mentioned that there was dictation software available to purchase and download in a home computer. I looked it up, downloaded it, and began to dictate God's miracles in my life.

A few weeks later, I began having chest pains. I even ended up going to the walk-in ER clinic one night because it hurt enough to make me fear a heart attack. It ended up being inflammation along the joint that connects the sternum to the rib cage. Costochondritis is what the term is called. It would hurt to breathe, making dictation very difficult. Again, I just laugh at the attempts that Satan has tried. They are obvious at this point, and my God is so much bigger! I was able to get to my rheumatologist. She gave me a shot of steroids and numbing medicine straight into my rib cage, and I was able to continue without pain.

On another front, God had begun putting the issue of the sex trade industry in front of me through a variety of means. I remember telling a friend very specifically that it almost felt like I was Jonah at this point; everywhere I turned the sex trade industry was the highlighted ministry. I quit Bible studies because of this topic. If a class or group at church, or an organization I was in decided to adopt this issue as their main issue for ministry purposes, I would quit going. I wasn't ready for it to be brought before me.

Finally I surrendered to God's telling me stop running away. I began to allow the concept of trusting him and what he was doing with this ministry. I was fine up until this point just giving my testimony. That seemed to involve things sufficiently in the past. But when it came to active involvement in the sex trade freedom ministry, it felt like the wounds were too fresh. I felt that when other people would talk about the horrors of sex slavery, they would be talking about my wounding without even knowing it and I couldn't look them in the face. I would even get angry at them. I would be angry at people who wanted to help others who were caught in the horrors of sex slavery because, at that time, I felt left out in the rescue. What if a rescue ministry had found me? Maybe so much damage would not have been done.

God is sovereign and counts all of our tears. He saw every injustice done to me. I began to see that He Himself was my rescue. I also began to realize my anger at the awareness of this injustice was a scapegoat for my own pain at my loss and what I experienced.

That was one of the things that God used to help me realize He wanted me to do more in this ministry. I remember the Holy Spirit asking me how is it that I can feel contempt and anger towards the ministry wanting to do God's work?

Obviously my anger was misplaced. When I did finally decide to yield to what God was asking me to do regarding testimony and witness about my situation in New York City and all the miracles that he had done for me, I told a friend about it at her house after church one morning. Her roommate just happened to overhear us.

She casually walked in and said "well you know, if you mean it—that you're willing to let God use you to speak truth about your testimony regarding this—there is an *As Our Own* event coming up. You could speak at it if you want. We need a keynote speaker." I remember laughing in appreciation of the grace and humor of God. He wastes no time . . . not even a whole minute had gone by. That event was one of the five speaking opportunities that I mentioned before. For the last six months, ministry has been writing this book. And where God takes it from here . . .

AFTERWARD

If you have been in a situation like this, whether you were groomed or raped, once or repeatedly, I strongly encourage you to seek out Christian counseling. God has Freedom for You! I know the burden of shame, it is a crushing impossibility. It took me years of so much struggle to be able to breathe without that crushing weight. I want you to know right now these three things:

- God Loves You, no matter what, and that will never change.
- Shame is a lie from Satan. God does not deal in shame, He deals in instruction and restitution, convicting us of sin so that we might turn from it back to Him and be

free. "There is now no condemnation for those who are in Christ." Romans 8:1

- You can and will make it through this. If you don't see it now, just take my word for it and lean on my experience. I would be honored to help you carry this burden. Please see the blog for <u>Almost Sold</u> and leave me your story so that I, and others, may pray for you.

Now, to speak to those who have a loved one who has gone through this horror. Hang in there. I cannot imagine your side of the coin, but what I can tell you is that in my worst moments of PTSD, the best healing balm was simply to be told "I love you no matter what" and "You are O.K." I did not need magic words, so let the pressure to "fix" be lifted in Jesus' name.

To those who do not know someone personally who had endured this, nor been through it themselves, I give a special call to action! This is a scheme of the devil that is particularly damaging. It had been many years since my escape and I am still crying in my counselor's office at various times over new revelations. Seek out any of the multitude of aid groups, or start one yourself, and take action. One life saved in my book is worth a lifetime of work.

Thank you for reading my story.

ADDITIONAL INFORMATION

If you have not accepted Jesus Christ as your savior, He is lovingly waiting for you. Acknowledge that you cannot save yourself, ask Him to forgive you for your wrongdoings and any sin in your life, and ask Him to be the Lord over your life, yielding your heart to Him.

If you need more guidance, have questions, or are looking for more resources around God or sex slavery, please visit the blog for <u>Almost Sold</u>.

24847517R00068

Made in the USA
San Bernardino, CA
08 October 2015